In a World of my Own

In a World of my Own

Glenn D. Ford

In A World Of My Own
© 2024 Glenn D. Ford

All rights reserved. No part of this book may be reproduced, stored in a retrieval system, or transmitted in any form or by any means—electronic, mechanical, photocopying, recording, or otherwise—without the prior written permission of the author, except by a reviewer who may quote brief passages in a review.

Author: Glenn D. Ford

Title: In A World Of My Own

Images:
All images in this book are created by Glenn D. Ford and Sarah J. Ford.
All Photographs are from the Author's private collection and are used with permission.

Written Content:
All written words are copyright © 2024 Glenn D. Ford.

ISBN: 9798337682464
Imprint: Independently published

First Edition: 2024

Disclaimer:
This is a work of non-fiction. The author has recounted events and experiences to the best of their recollection. Names and identifying details have been changed to protect the privacy of individuals.

Cover Design by: Glenn D. Ford
Edited by: Sarah J. Ford

In a World of my Own

Glenn D. Ford

In A World Of My Own
© 2024 Glenn D. Ford

All rights reserved. No part of this book may be reproduced, stored in a retrieval system, or transmitted in any form or by any means—electronic, mechanical, photocopying, recording, or otherwise—without the prior written permission of the author, except by a reviewer who may quote brief passages in a review.

Author: Glenn D. Ford

Title: In A World Of My Own

Images:
All images in this book are created by Glenn D. Ford and Sarah J. Ford.
All Photographs are from the Author's private collection and are used with permission.

Written Content:
All written words are copyright © 2024 Glenn D. Ford.

ISBN: 9798337682464
Imprint: Independently published

First Edition: 2024

Disclaimer:
This is a work of non-fiction. The author has recounted events and experiences to the best of their recollection. Names and identifying details have been changed to protect the privacy of individuals.

Cover Design by: Glenn D. Ford
Edited by: Sarah J. Ford

To my Grandparents:
Albert and Beatrice Ford,
Frank and Daisy Thorpe
And
My Mum and Dad.

To Friends and Family and Lisa, a lady in a cafe I sometimes frequent, and my local vet. For giving me some words of encouragement, others proof reading and giving me constructive feedback. I am most grateful.

To my Granddaughter Sarah, without whose guidance with the ins and outs of the computer this book would never have seen the light of day. Thank you for also typing it all up for me and dealing with all the edits I would bring to you.

To my Wife, for putting up with me for over 50 years, it can't have been an easy experience, as I flit from painting and writing and watching football every spare moment. And spending time with our dogs, there always has to be dogs in the home.

Contents

Chapter 1: Half The World Away 1

Chapter 2: Nomadic Schooldays 9

Chapter 3: The Grand Prix Season Begins 15

Chapter 4: Nostalgic Delights 29

Chapter 5: The Italian Showdown 37

Chapter 6: Culinary Treats and Football Fandom 47

Chapter 7: Cricketing Chess Match 61

Chapter 8: Thrills and Spills on the Imaginary Turf 69

Chapter 9: Childhood Battles 81

Chapter 10: Cowboy Town Confrontation 95

Chapter 11: The Iconic Streets of Monaco 103

Chapter 12: Unforgettable Triumphs and Rock & Roll 113

Chapter 13: Sports Galore 119

Chapter 14: Golden Age of Television 125

Chapter 15: A Year of Cinematic Wonder 131

References 145

About the Author 147

When I think of my Gramp, I am immediately transported to a world of vivid colours, boundless imagination, and the comforting warmth of his stories. Growing up, I was captivated by the tales he shared, each one more enchanting than the last. It is with immense pride and joy that I write this foreword to his debut autobiography, "In A World of my Own."

Glenn's story is a tapestry woven from the threads of a remarkable life. Born in 1955, he has worn many hats over the years—shop worker, office clerk, factory labourer, and care provider. Yet, beyond these roles, he has always been more than his professions. He is a devoted husband, a loving father, and a proud grandad, roles he embraces with unparalleled enthusiasm and love.

As an artist, Glenn has always found solace and expression through his creative pursuits. His passion for art is evident in every page of this book, where his words paint pictures as vividly as his brushstrokes. Football, too, has been a lifelong love, a sport that has brought him joy and camaraderie throughout the years.

This autobiography is not just a recounting of events; it is an invitation to step into Glenn's world, to see life through his eyes, and to experience the wonder and imagination that have defined his journey. It is a testament to his creativity, dedication, and the indomitable spirit that has shaped his life.

As his granddaughter, I have had the privilege of witnessing firsthand the incredible person he is. "In A World of my Own" is more than a book; it is a piece of his heart and soul, a gift to all who read it. I invite you to embark on this journey with him, to explore the world he has so lovingly crafted, and to be inspired by the magic that lies within.

With love and admiration,
Sarah J. Ford

Chapter 1: Half The World Away

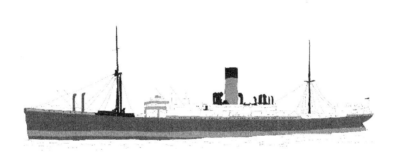

1964 Idyllic Childhood Days

Now my life was full of television, pop music, toys, and sports.

I knew very little of what was happening in the real world of adults.

At 8 years and 8 months old, I was living in a dream, a sort of idyllic childhood fantasy world.

There was always music playing in our house, but mostly it was playing in my head. Even now I can hear The Beatles 'I Want to Hold Your Hand'. I would be playing out different scenes from films, football and cricket matches that I had glimpsed on the TV screen, as I slipped into a world of my own.

BBC's Grandstand programme introduced me to many different superstars who I would use to take part in my imaginary games. Although these games were played out on the sitting room floor or hallway, not on the famous pitches of Wembley, Old Trafford, Anfield, or my favourite White Hart Lane. I could only dream of stepping out onto the hallowed turf of Lords or Wimbledon. Aintree only appeared once a year on our television screens, and horse racing was a long way away from the dice game I had made to hold my own Grand National.

Images of the huge fences like Valentines and Beechers Brook were drawn on a Snakes and Ladders board. I was forever changing and making things. Once getting hold of my Dad's playing cards. When he next went to play with them, he turned to me and wanted to know why I had written all over the cards. I explained that the words Caught, Stumped, Not Out, Bowled, LBW and Extras were all part of a new Cricket game I had made up. Lucky for me, Dad had a fresh pack he could use, which he then kept out of the drawer and well away from my scribblings.

In reality, my Horse Racing Escalado set was nothing like the Epsom Derby that I had created. There was no end to where my mind could take me around the sporting arena. Setting myself up with my bits and bobs, transporting me to a make-believe world. Always having a pen and paper on hand to set the rules.

Let's go back to the very beginning. I was born in Sleaford, Lincolnshire on the 25th of April 1955 to Ronald and Lilian Ford. It would be over six years before we became a family of four when my sister Melanie arrived.

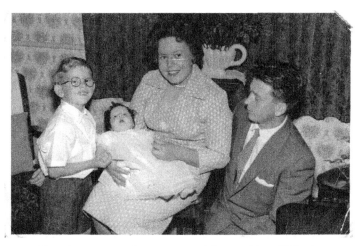

Me and my sister with our parents: Lilian and Ronald Ford

Dad was in the RAF and within 3 months of my birth, he was posted to Hong Kong. One month later myself and my Mum would join him.

What an adventure that was to be. Unknown to me at the time, my 19-year-old Mum and I would take a slow boat to China.

We left Lincoln for Liverpool to board the ship to take us on our travels. Grandad Frank, Mum's father, cried his eyes out, begging her not to go. I have always felt a special fondness for Liverpool. Perhaps travelling through the Mersey Tunnel as a baby could have had something to do with that.

On the 26th of August 1955, we set sail on the Anchises, a Blue Funnel Line 1st Class Ship. I always wonder if it could have been possible that a 14-year-old John Lennon bunking off school was at Liverpool docks that day watching the ships set off on their journeys to far-off lands. Waving me and my Mum off, perhaps I was the original 'Bonnie'. Thirteen passengers were on board, two destined for Singapore, three for Port Swettenham, Malaysia and another four for Penang, with four of us set for Hong Kong.

The journey would take 5 weeks and 1 day. Ten days at sea without seeing land until we reached Gibraltar.

Out into the Mediterranean, through to the Suez Canal, onto the Red Sea. Mum told me stories of how she looked through her cabin porthole and how she could have almost touched the Arabian people on their camels that were watching our passage.

A pilot from our ship had to guide us through the dangerous waters.

Onto the Indian Ocean and then the China seas. It was then Kowloon and Hong Kong Harbour.

Again, Mum spoke of the wonderful breathtaking sight of all the boats everywhere.

On a stopover in Singapore, she was given a tour around the island and went to the Raffles Bar with the Ship's captain who had hired a car for the outing.

On board the ship, Mum said she spent many nights dining at the captain's table. What an experience that must have been travelling halfway around the world in 36 days. It would be just over 3 years before we were back in England.

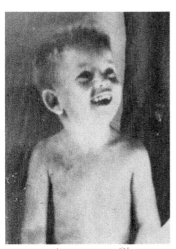
A very young Glenn

In Hong Kong, as a baby I spent a lot of time with the local Chinese people in the nearby streets eating with them, and apparently speaking Chinese before I could speak English. Because my hair was blonde, I was patted and touched on my head for luck and good fortune.

We lived on the RAF Camp in Kai Tak. This was to be my Dad's favourite posting and to be my Mum's happiest time of her life. She was treated like a princess and waited on hand and foot, spending lots of time on the beach and taking refreshing dips in the inviting water.

My Mum

Whilst in Hong Kong, my Dad represented the RAF in Boxing Matches. One particular fight he told me about was against a local Chinese Champion.

After the first two rounds of the bout, Dad was certain he was winning on points with the final round to come. He thought it was to be his day. Having won a lot of his previous fights, he felt good and strong.

The Bell sounded for the third round, and the Chinaman went wild and belted my Dad round the Boxing Ring to win on a points decision.

A gutsy performance from Dad, but he obviously met his match that day. He said it was like fighting a crazy madman.

I had an Amah maid (Nanny) who looked after me all day. Her name was Ayling. I went everywhere with her, whilst she coped with me and the housekeeping, carrying me around as she worked.

Me and Ayling

When it was time to leave Hong Kong, we all travelled back to England on a BOAC flight, a time that takes us back to a different era when air travel was still a novelty, every journey holding an air of adventure and true excitement. This trip took us four days with stopovers for refuelling at Karachi, Pakistan, Basra in Iraq, and Rome, Italy, finally landing at Gatwick Airport.

I have a faint recollection of sitting on the floor of the Airplane beside my Mum and Dad having a meal from a plastic tray with different sections in it. I don't recall what I had to eat.

Cheers from Me, Mum and Dad

Chapter 2: Nomadic Schooldays

By 1964, I had attended four different primary schools. It was always the same. If I didn't have a place to sit in the classroom, I would be placed in a seat for a child who was not at school that day, probably because of illness. When they returned, I would be moved again. This process would go on until eventually I would be found a permanent place. This would go on every time at every school. I got used to it and I suppose it made me interact with other children in class because I sat with most of them at some time or another. It was quite a nomadic life being the child of an Airforce Parent.

In the short time between 1958 and 1964, Dad was stationed at three RAF Stations. RAF Digby in Lincolnshire, RAF Yatesbury in Wiltshire, RAF Brampton in Cambridgeshire.

We lived in Calne, a small town in Wiltshire for a short time. We then moved close by to the village of Yatesbury again for a short stay eventually settling in Marlborough on the High Street above a Fish and Chip shop. Every week Mum took me to the local Toy Shop, where I would choose a couple of toy cowboys or indians for my collection from the large glass display cabinet. We spent many happy hours in that wonderful magical emporium.

Dad was working as a Chef on the camp as he worked at R.A.F. Yatesbury. We didn't always live on the Camp itself, hence all the moving and different schools.

It was a lovely part of the Country and the White Horse on Cherhill Down was a smashing spot for a picnic. I remember going there with my Mum and Dad with our blanket and prepared feast, ham sandwiches, egg and cress sandwiches, sausage rolls. cheese cut in small chunks, Cakes, Lemonade, and a Flask of Tea. No lashings of ginger beer thankfully, I didn't like ginger beer the one time I tried it, I was left with a bitter after taste in my mouth. The whole thing was like a banquet, a meal fit for a King.

I vividly recall rolling a small way down the hill and my Dad following me down making sure I came to no harm; it was all good fun.

The Horse was cut into the hill 175 years before I was born in 1780 when the turf was stripped away to reveal the chalk underneath, well that's according to my teacher.

My memories of primary school life are very vague, I would imagine it was because I went to so many schools in such a short space of time, most of my experiences would have been taken up with meeting new children and teachers in another different environment as no school would be the same.

On the odd occasion, my education would be ahead, but often as not, I would move and I would be behind with my studies, as education was taught at different rates in different places.

Corporal punishment was handed out even in Primary School, and I vividly remember having to stand in line with some other children for what would have been a small misdemeanour, talking in class, fidgeting in a chair, basically anything that annoyed the teacher.

I would get my two strokes of the cane from the Headmistress, and you held your hand out to receive your punishment and was careful to keep your thumb in, because being hit on the thumb was far more painful than the cane across the palm. I was once given the slipper in front of the whole class, I had to lay across the Teachers desk on my front, with the "This is going to hurt you boy" he smacked me hard across my buttocks, to be fair this was the easiest punishment because it hardly hurt at all and it took a lot not to laugh as I went back to my seat. This all makes me sound like a bad pupil, but I wasn't. It was just the normality of the day.

When I got home and was asked by my Mum what sort of day I had, I would tell the truth about the awful beating I had taken, for her to say "Well, you must have done something really bad", but the truth was nine times out of ten, I hadn't. Still, it was part of growing up and I just got on with it.

One really nice memory I have of primary school was being in the classroom for a Mathematics lesson. I just wish I could recall the Teacher's name. I just can't. He was fun and seemed to be smiling all the time, he wasn't as grim as some.

We were all at our seats, I was sitting about eight rows back from the Blackboard, safe from board rubber throwing, I could see it a mile off from there. In walked Mr Tortoise. I'm going to call him that because that's what he used to do.

We all stood up to greet him, Hello Mr Tortoise, Hello Children he replied, his eyes intently staring directly at me.

My first thought was that I hadn't done anything wrong, especially as this was the start of the lesson. There hadn't been enough time to get into trouble. Still, he stared at me, "sit down everyone", he said, "not you Glenn Ford."

I want you to go into that space away from your chair, he said pointing with his finger to where he wanted me to stand. I did as he asked and just stood there not knowing why. Now everyone in the class had their eyes fixed on me.

Suddenly his right hand pulled back the front of his jacket and he placed his hand as if he was taking something from his pocket. He then said in a booming voice "So you think you are the Fastest Gun Alive, well go for it." That's when I quickly realised, I was in the middle of an imaginary Cowboy Gunfight. I went for my imaginary gun, unfortunately he was quicker and with a loud bang he claimed that he had shot the gun out of my hand and claimed to be the Fastest Gun Alive.

What a way to start the day, he explained to the rest of the class that he had been watching a film the previous night at home on television. The main star of the film just happened to be Glenn Ford. I was famous in that Maths class for a while until a lad called John Wayne turned up, I think his real name was John Morrison really, The Teacher called him Wayne.

Chapter 3: The Grand Prix Season Begins.

The news headlines interrupt the Swinging Blue Jeans song 'Hippy, Hippy Shake.'

NEWS HEADLINES

Robert Kennedy US Attorney General flies to Tokyo as a special envoy, to meet President Sukarno of Indonesia, in an attempt to calm the Indonesian hostilities towards Malaysia.

It seems that there is a lot of violence happening around the world.

In Cyprus, hostilities are carrying on between Greek and Turkish Cypriot communities.

In Malaysia, British and Gurkha forces are active along the borders of Borneo, Sarawak, and Sabah.

In Accra Ghana, an attempt to assassinate President Nkrumah fails.

Western Berliners have been allowed to visit relatives in East Berlin. It was all sealed again after a very short period.

Contract by a British firm to sell buses to Cuba causes criticism in the USA.

British officers in Dar-es-Salaam faced a mutiny from a battalion of Tanganyika Rifles.

British troops flown in as unrest in the Ugandan army.

Trouble in Kenya, British troops called in.

Paddy Hopkirk won the Monte Carlo Rally in a Mini Cooper.

President De Gaulle of France announces recognition of Communist China.

The Winter Olympics open in Innsbruck, Austria.

Actor Alan Ladd has passed away at the age of 56.

U.S. launches Ranger 6 to relay televised close-up pictures of the moon's surface before crash landing.

Once the News headlines had finished, it was back to the music and the voice of Gene Pitney and his Twenty-four hours from Tulsa.

My Corgi and Dinky cars were in two large biscuit tins, which were kept in a cupboard under the stairs.

There were all sorts of things in there, including old half tins of paint, and the smell from them would linger in the air for a short while when I opened that door.

First Race of the Year

It was the start of my Grand Prix Season. I decided on eight races in all. Starting with the Austrian Grand Prix, there wouldn't be much difference in each race on the Grand Prix Calendar.

I would take a different route around the house with each race. I am going through the knees of another pair of long school trousers. The small hole that has appeared is getting bigger and my Mum won't be best pleased, and it will have to be patched.

As I crawl around the sitting room floor, the swirling patterned red carpet looks like a racetrack and there is even a chicane woven into it.

So, Twenty Cars have been picked out alongside 20 drivers, all the details are carefully written into an Exercise Book, all neatly done.

Staying away from the out-of-bounds areas, especially the stereogram and television, but I still have the bridge and underpass which is in fact the coffee table.

This particular first race was over six laps of the room; each car and van would be given a gentle push in turn.

Any vehicle which unfortunately had the misfortune of crashing, which would result in it laying on its side, would be withdrawn from the race and placed back in one of the tins.

After all the cars had their initial push, places would then be determined, then the whole process would continue, with the vehicle in front being pushed first and so on.

Before the race commenced, there was a ritual of all the Drivers queuing up for a traditional 99 ice cream with a chocolate flake, the reason this strange happening took place was because one of the twenty participants was Trevor Taylor, who would be driving an Ice-Cream Van this year. The man in the back of the van serving was his lead mechanic.

It may have been the wish of many of the drivers to have an alternative to the 'Ninety-Nine', a more appropriate treat would have been an Ice Lolly ZOOM!

Me and that lolly

Whenever I imagined these races and played them out, I would loudly commentate what was happening, sometimes to the annoyance of my parents.

19

List of the participants:

John Surtees (GB) would be in the red Shark Nose Ferrari in his white overalls and helmet, Racing Number 36 in white on the side. He is at home on two wheels as well as on four.

Jim Clark (GB) the Scotsman and current World Champion, is in a Blue Lotus, kitted out in a white helmet and the Number One displayed on the bonnet.

Gerhard Mitter (GER) is normally a part of team Lotus, but today in a white Ford Zephyr Police Car, Motorway Patrol with a red interior and an Aerial, plus a blue beacon.

Mike Hailwood (GB) 'Mike the Bike' driving a black Riley Pathfinder with a Beacon on its roof. Police Siren and Aerial.

Jo Siffert (SWI) 'Seppi' to his friends in a Red Citroen DS19 with a yellow interior.

Bob Anderson (GB) normally driving his own Lola, today in the red Austin Seven with light yellow interior.

Graham Hill (GB) in the Green BRM with a Number 3 on the side. Graham sat in the cockpit, overalls, and helmet on. The Former World Champion worked into the night helping prepare the car before the race.

Trevor Taylor (GB) in the Mister Softee Ice-Cream Van with Ice Cream man inside behind the sliding windows. He would usually be driving a Lotus Climax, so he may well find this out of his comfort zone.

Mike Spence (GB) Lotus Driver, today in a yellow Bedford AA Road Services van with black roof.

Jack Brabham (AUS) Cooper driver, today in a yellow Aston Martin DB4. Two-time World Champion.

Lorenzo Bandini (IT) in a Ford Anglia, pale green in colour with a red interior. More well known for driving for Ferrari.

Phil Hill (USA) is in a black and white Sheriff's Oldsmobile with a star on the front door and a red beacon. As a Ferrari Driver, he is a Former World Champion.

Tony Maggs (SA) in a red Jaguar Fire Chief Van with a yellow interior. He is the first South African to participate in a Formula One Grand Prix.

Innes Ireland (GB) in a two-tone grey Rolls Royce Silver Wraith. He is a former Rolls Royce Engineer.

Richie Ginther (USA) the star from Hollywood, California in a red Vanwall with the Number 25 on it.

Chris Amon (NZ) hoping for his luck to change for his first Grand Prix Victory in a grey Hillman Imp with a white interior.

Dan Gurney (USA) Whether it is winning in Sports Cars or Nascar, Dan is taking to the red Alfa Romeo with the Number 8 on it, grey tyres and the driver wearing a white helmet to this Grand Prix.

Jo Bonnier (SWE) is the first Swede to enter and win a Formula One Grand Prix. He is hopeful today in a Fiat in Mauve/Pink, a Venetian blind in the back window and a brown roof.

Bruce McLaren (NZ) is a Race Car Designer and Inventor in a light blue Ford Consul Cortina with a beige interior.

Peter Arundell (GB) gives up his Lotus for the RAF Vanguard Staff car. This fits in line with his time in the RAF to becoming a professional Race Car Driver.

Racing Commentary:

As the race begins, I can hear the sound of The Searchers song, Needles, and Pins, coming from the kitchen radio.

By now, a warm sun was shining through the window and in my mind, I could see the surrounding mountains and greenery, and not the usual dull circuit.

The flag was raised as Clark and Brabham led from the front ahead of Bonnier and Ireland.

The tail-enders Taylor and Anderson got off to a slow start.

Brabham set the pace with Clark and Ireland right behind him, then Bonnier, Siffert and Amon made up the front six.

At last Clark took the lead, only for him to spin out of control and put himself out of the race, and Brabham and Ireland sped past him.

The two swapped 1st and 2nd place many times as the race developed.

3rd place was now solely owned by Amon and leaving Bonnier and Siffert in his wake.

At the halfway stage, the order was: Ireland, Brabham, Amon, Siffert and then the rest. The race lost one more to retirement, the car of Bonnier.

Siffert was the next to fail, and he had to pull out of the race.

With 2 laps remaining, Ireland looked all set for a win with a considerate lead over Brabham.

Slowly but surely Brabham eventually caught up with Ireland and sailed past him to the eventual 1st place spot and takes the chequered flag with Amon moving into finishing 2nd place.

Ireland was struggling on the final lap but managed to hold off the chasing pack for 3rd place: 4th G. Hill, 5th Ginther, 6th Surtees, 7th Gurney, and 8th McLaren.

Way back down the circuit, the strugglers still managed to finish the race: in 9th place P. Hill, 10th Arundel, 11th Anderson, 12th Spence, 13th Hailwood, 14th Taylor, 15th Mitter, 16th Bandini, and 17th Maggs.

17 drivers of the starting 20 finished the race.

The points system for each race is as follows:

1st Place   -   8 points

2nd Place   -   6 Points

3rd Place   -   4 Points

4th Place   -   3 Points

5th Place   -   2 Points

6th Place   -   1 Point

Brabham is in an Aston Martin DB4, Amon in a Hillman Imp and Ireland in a Rolls Royce they head for the podium, I can hear the sound of the Dave Clark 5 song Glad All Over playing.

Race 2

German Grand Prix Result

Place	Driver	Car
1	Surtees	Shark Nose Ferrari
2	Clark	Lotus
3	Ginther	Vanwall
4	Arundell	RAF Vanguard Staff Car
5	Brabham	Aston Martin DB4
6	Siffert	Citroen DS19
7	Anderson	Austin Seven
8	Spence	Bedford AA Road Services Van
9	Bonnier	Fiat
10	Phil Hill	Sheriffs Oldsmobile
11	Hailwood	Riley Pathfinder
12	Taylor	Mister Softee Ice-Cream Van
13	Mitter	Ford Zephyr Police Car

Retired from Race	
Driver	Car
Maggs	Jaguar Fire Chief Van
Gurney	Alfa Romeo
McLaren	Ford Consul Cortina
Graham Hill	BRM
Amon	Hillman Imp
Ireland	Rolls Royce Silver Wraith
Bandini	Ford Anglia

Driver Standings (after 2 races)

Place	Driver	Car	Points
1st	Brabham	Aston Martin DB4	10
2nd	Surtees	Shark Nose Ferrari	9
3rd	Amon	Hillman Imp	6
	Clark	Lotus	6
	Ginther	Vanwall	6
6th	Ireland	Rolls Royce Silver Wraith	4
7th	Arundell	RAF Vanguard Staff Car	3
	G Hill	BRM	3
9th	Siffert	Citroen DS19	1

Chapter 4: Nostalgic Delights

The news headlines interrupt Cilla Black singing Anyone Who Had a Heart.

NEWS HEADLINES

Tony Nash and Robin Dixon win Britain's First Gold Medal at the Innsbruck Winter Olympics in the two-man bobsleigh event.

Lidija Skoblikova, a Russian speed skater, won her fourth Olympic Gold Medal in just four days, setting a new record.

Bombs have exploded at the US embassy in Nicosia, Cyprus, prompting the evacuation of American women and children.

The British and French governments are moving forward with joint agreements to construct a Channel Railway Tunnel.

Amidst a frenzy of excitement, The Beatles made their grand debut in New York, captivating enthusiastic crowds.

This year marks the 400th anniversary of Galileo's birth, the renowned Italian astronomer, physicist, and engineer.

The trial of Jack Ruby, who is charged with the murder of Lee Harvey Oswald, has commenced.

The 400th Anniversary of Michelangelo's death, the Italian sculptor, painter, and architect.

Picture by Rubens, titled 'Negro Heads' and valued at £70,000, was stolen from a gallery in Brussels.

The UN Security Council starts discussions on Cyprus.

Legendary actor Peter Sellers ties the knot with the beautiful Britt Eckland.

At London Airport, an impressive crowd of 10,000 fervent fans has eagerly assembled to joyously celebrate the long-awaited return of The Beatles to Britain.

Henry Cooper gains the European Heavyweight Boxing title when he defeats Brian London on points in Manchester.

Cassius Clay becomes Heavyweight Boxing Champion of the world, stopping Sonny Liston in six rounds at Miami Beach, Florida.

Once the News headlines had finished, it was back to the music and the voice of the wonderful Irish Trio of the Bachelors with their song Diane.

As I said before, my early school days are just vague blurred times. I know I went to school, but my memories are more about home life. Why I can vividly remember Mondays being Washday, I do not know why, but smells have stayed in my head and the distinct smell of Tide lingering in the air and still lingers in my mind.

Tuesday was Baking Day, and the cakes were plain but delicious, they were always topped with icing. The Chocolate cake, so moist and so inviting to eat, is cut into squares with chocolate icing poured on top and the Vanilla cake covered in white icing. The smell and taste of those cakes being sweet, soft, and delicious.

What happened during the other weekdays has now faded from my memory, but I do remember the Corona Man delivering bottles, Limeade, Cream Soda, Cherryade, Lemonade and my particular favourite Orangeade.

They stood there in the morning like soldiers standing on guard on our doorstep.

On Saturday, a lady with a van used to turn up with an array of groceries and goodies.

I could not believe what I was seeing placed in front of me, all my very favourite sweets and chocolates.

My Mum and Auntie Joyce were picking out the Typhoo Tea packets, the Blue Band Margarine, Kellogg's Cornflakes, Tins of Carnation Milk, Robertson's Jam in different varieties, Tunnock's Tea Cakes were there, we always ate well.

I was only really interested at that moment in what I could buy with my pocket money. How could I possibly decide what to have? The colours of the wrappers and packets were enough to send your head into a spin.

The list of delights was almost endless: Toffee Crisp, Wine Gums, Picnic, Aniseed Balls, Love Hearts, Smarties, Munchies, Fruit Gums, Milk Chocolate Buttons, Aero, Sherbert Fountains, Milky Way, Opal Fruits, Spangles, Bubble-gum, Milky Bars.

Surely there can't be anymore, but there in a second basket, was filled to the brim with: Fruit Pastilles, Polo's, Bourneville Bars, Turkish Delight, Gobstoppers, Black Jacks, Fruit and Nut, Bountys, Fruit Salad Sweets, Crunchie Bars, Rolo's, Maltesers, Caramac, Five Boys Chocolate, Flakes, and my favourite Mars Bars.

One moment I do remember from my first day at Primary School was getting told off for singing in class. I was always singing at home.

The song was "Standing on the Corner, watching all the girls go by."

It was an old tune written a year after I was born, but I remember hearing it one time on the television programme, 'The Sunday Night at the London Palladium.' It was sung by the Dallas Boys.

The Dallas Boys who came from Leicester, the five piece vocal group, possibly Britain's first boy band, always made me think of a hand. To me, they looked a bit like the four fingers and a thumb, due to their silhouette on the stage. Strange how things can imprint on the mind of a child, well, at least this child.

I can hear Billy J Kramer and the Dakotas Little Children and the Beatles Can't Buy Me Love drifting through the house.

NEWS HEADLINES

Fresh outbreak of hostilities between Turkish and Greek Cypriots on the west coast of Cyprus involving British troops.

A third son, Edward, is born to Queen Elizabeth 11

Turkish ships were put to sea just off the coast of Cyprus.

A party of Canadian peacekeepers arrive in Cyprus.

In Dallas, Texas, Jack Ruby is found guilty of murdering Lee Harvey Oswald.

Legendary Hollywood icon Elizabeth Taylor ties the knot with the charming Richard Burton.

Grand National at Aintree is won by Team Spirit on four previous occasions, an unsuccessful runner in the same race.

At Aylesbury, Bucks, the trial of 11 men arrested after the Great Train Robbery of August 8th, 1962, ends. All are found guilty.

Teenage Gangs invade Clacton Essex on motorcycles, 97 arrests made after rioting and hooliganism.

Cambridge wins 110th University Boat Race by 6 ½ lengths.

The music resumes with the lively Bits and Pieces by the Dave Clark 5 and The Hollies with Just One Look

Chapter 5: The Italian Showdown

Race 3

Dutch Grand Prix Result

Place	Driver	Car
1	Clark	Lotus
2	Gurney	Alfa Romeo
3	Surtees	Shark Nose Ferrari
4	Ginther	Vanwall
5	Hailwood	Riley Pathfinder
6	Ireland	Rolls Royce Silver Wraith
7	Spence	Bedford AA Road Services Van
8	Taylor	Mister Softee Ice-Cream Van
9	Siffert	Citroen DS19
10	Bandini	Ford Anglia
11	Arundell	RAF Vanguard Staff Car

Retired from Race	
Driver	Car
G. Hill	BRM
Brabham	Aston Martin DB4
Bonnier	Fiat
Amon	Hillman Imp
P. Hill	Sheriffs Oldsmobile
Maggs	Jaguar Fire Chief Van
McLaren	Ford Consul Cortina
Mitter	Ford Zephyr Police Car
Anderson	Austin Seven

Drivers' Standings after 3 Races

Place	Driver	Car	Points
1st	Clark	Lotus	14
2nd	Surtees	Shark Nose Ferrari	13
3rd	Brabham	Aston Martin DB4	10
4th	Ginther	Vanwall	9
5th	Amon	Hillman Imp	6
	Gurney	Alfa Romeo	6
7th	Ireland	Rolls Royce Silver Wraith	5
8th	G. Hill	BRM	3
	Arundell	RAF Vanguard Staff Car	3
10th	Hailwood	Riley Pathfinder	2
11th	Siffert	Citroen DS19	1

4th Race

Italian Grand Prix

The circuit was bathed in warm sunshine as the flag dropped for the 4th race of the season.

Jim Clark and Graham Hill were side by side at the front with John Surtees tucked in just behind to make a 3-way tie for the lead.

A gap quickly opened up to the rest of the drivers, headed by Dan Gurney and Lorenzo Bandini, Trevor Taylor, Peter Arundell, and Bob Anderson, who filled the next three places.

By the second lap Surtees and Clark began to pull away, Graham Hill having dropped back to the chasing pack, which was now headed by Ginther with Gurney and Bandini close.

A third group of Brabham, McLaren, Bonnier, and Ireland interchanged with each other several times.

Back to the lead, Surtees in his Red Ferrari was weaving his way in front, but Clark, in the blue Lotus, was close by. This was becoming an epic tussle between the two leaders.

Then suddenly Surtees had an unfortunate engine failure and had to withdraw from the race, leaving Clark well clear of the field at the halfway stage.

Second place was now Gurney's Alfa Romeo with Graham Hill in the Green BRM in 3rd and a long way back Ginther's Vanwall, Bandini's Ford Anglia, Ireland's Rolls Royce, and Brabham's Aston Martin.

Jo Siffert's Red Citroen entered the pits and did not return to the race.

Further down the field were Phil Hill, Mitter, Spence and Maggs.

With only two laps remaining, both Amon and Hailwood limped their Hillman Imp and Riley Pathfinder into the pits to retire.

Gurney and Graham Hill slipped back into the back markers with Ireland fading as well, the race having taken its toll.

The final lap was truly on, with Ginther gaining ground every second, to the front 3 of Clark, Bandini, and Brabham.

He forced his way past Brabham and was now chasing hard on the front two.

It was an exciting finish as Clark headed Bandini approaching the final bend. Ginther made his move on that turn and flashed past both cars to take the chequered flag. Clark finished second with Bandini a gallant third.

Race 4

Italian Grand Prix Result

Place	Driver	Car
1	Ginther	Vanwall
2	Clark	Lotus
3	Bandini	Ford Anglia
4	Brabham	Aston Martin DB4
5	P. Hill	Sheriffs Oldsmobile
6	Spence	Bedford AA Road Services Van
7	Mitter	Ford Zephyr Police Car
8	Bonnier	Fiat
9	Maggs	Jaguar Fire Chief Van
10	Gurney	Alfa Romeo
11	Taylor	Mister Softee Ice-Cream Van
12	Arundell	RAF Vanguard Staff Car
13	McLaren	Ford Consul Cortina
14	G. Hill	BRM
15	Ireland	Rolls Royce Silver Wraith
16	Anderson	Austin Seven

Retired from Race	
Driver	**Car**
Siffert	Citroen DS19
Surtees	Shark Nose Ferrari
Amon	Hillman Imp
Hailwood	Riley Pathfinder

Driver Standings after 4 races

Place	Driver	Car	Points
1st	Clark	Lotus	20
2nd	Ginther	Vanwall	17
3rd	Brabham	Aston Martin DB4	13
	Surtees	Shark Nose Ferrari	13
5th	Amon	Hillman Imp	6
	Gurney	Alfa Romeo	6
7th	Ireland	Rolls Royce Silver Wraith	5
8th	Bandini	Ford Anglia	4
9th	G. Hill	BRM	3
	Arundell	RAF Vanguard Staff Car	3
11th	P. Hill	Sheriffs Oldsmobile	2
	Hailwood	Riley Pathfinder	2
13th	Siffert	Citroen DS19	1
	Spence	Bedford AA Road Services Van	1

NEWS HEADLINES

Death of General Douglas MacArthur, U.S. Army's Supreme Commander, in the Second World War against Japan 1941-45 and First Commander of UN Forces in Korea 1950-51.

In the aftermath of the Great Train Robbery, all 12 men who were found guilty in connection with the crime were handed substantial prison sentences as a punishment for their involvement.

The 400th Anniversary of William Shakespeare's birth is celebrated.

Liverpool became the champions of the 1963/64 Football League by defeating Arsenal 5-0.

Explosion and fire at Battersea Power Station and a cable fault in Buckinghamshire cause four-hour power failure across London, wrecking the much announced opening of BBC2 TV Service.

From the kitchen radio, the sound of Peter and Gordon's 'World Without Love' followed by Milly with 'My Boy Lollipop'. Time for one more hit as I daydream the day away, The Searchers 'Don't Throw Your Love Away'

Chapter 6: Culinary Treats and Football Fandom

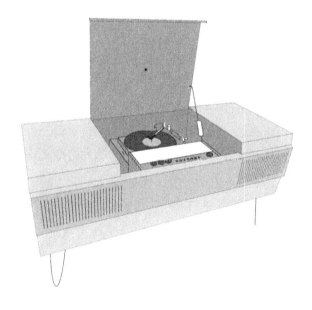

I also enjoyed eating my meals, but one meal I just couldn't have was liver. I hated the stuff. The mere thought of it would make me want to be sick. It wasn't the taste initially; it was that awful smell.

When I was at school for school meals, it was served up with bacon.

I loved Bacon, but again I couldn't eat it, no matter how many times I tried to explain to the cooks and dinner ladies, "You have cooked the bacon with the liver and now it just smells of liver, and the thought of it would make me gag".

I had my Sunday dinner prepared and cooked by my Mum and Dad.

My Dad was a chef, and my Mum was also a very good cook.

Sunday Dinner was always a roast with all the trimmings. It could be chicken, pork, lamb, or beef. It would regularly change week by week.

Roast potatoes, mashed potatoes, carrots, and maybe some peas, sometimes cabbage or some other green vegetable, stuffing if it was chicken, Yorkshire pudding with the beef, a bread sauce which was so creamy with onions and mushrooms, all topped with a wonderful gravy.

While we ate the meal, the radio on the stereogram would be tuned to 2 Way Family Favourites with Jean Metcalfe and Cliff Michelmore.

We were big fans of the show, probably because we were a Force's Family.

Messages from Germany, Aden, Cyprus, Hong Kong and many more places, from members of the Navy, Army and Airforce bases spread out across the world, sending song requests and messages to loved ones, which rang out over the airwaves.

Two other programmes I can remember on the Radio, the first being my favourite The Clitheroe Kid starring Jimmy Clitheroe. He played the part of a cheeky schoolboy and lived with his family in Lilac Avenue somewhere Up North.

The main storyline for the show was mostly about misunderstandings as Jimmy would be overhearing conversations and often getting the wrong end of the stick. He would nearly always be involved in a money-making scheme to make his pocket money go further.

The humour was particularly sarcastic as Jimmy was always giving people in his life nicknames, Teachers, Friends, and Family but not his mother who he worshipped. His catchphrase "Don't some mothers 'ave 'em!" used to make me laugh.

The other programme was the Navy Lark, this would be playing on the radio, and I would hear bits and pieces of it, as the different voices sounded so funny. The main Actors in the show were Jon Pertwee, Leslie Phillips, Stephen Murray, and Ronnie Barker. It was set on board the H.M.S. Troutbridge a British Royal Navy Frigate based in Portsmouth I didn't understand all the humour from that show it was more something Dad would laugh at.

Still, what a warm feeling that gives me as I drift back to hear the Four Pennies 'Juliet', and Cilla Black's 'You're My World'.

After dinner, I would borrow my Dad's newspaper, the News of The Word. Sometimes it was The People, and I would look intensely at the football reports.

The thing that always fascinated me was the team listings at the end of each match report.

This was the beginning of my education of the Beautiful Game.

I would study every detail to see who had played the previous day. I always made a mental note of every first division player.

I became so obsessed that I knew each player better than I knew my own family members.

I would collect cigarette cards. I don't know where they all came from, probably from my Grandad and Dad. It was a mystery to me, but I was so grateful to receive them.

I would sort out my favourites and lay the cards out in their positions, forming several teams.

I vividly remember certain cards. The Goalkeepers were Gordon Banks. Banks joined Chesterfield in 1953 before I was born and he played in the 1956 F.A. Youth Cup Final. He was sold to. Leicester City for £7,000 in 1959. He played in the 1961 and 1963 F.A. Cup Finals, losing on both occasions.

Made his England debut in 1963, the same year he was chosen to play against the Rest of the World team in a match to celebrate the 100 years of the Football Association. This time, he was on the winning side.

All this information, or most of it, was on the back of the cigarette card, the front showing a picture of him.

Other Keepers that come to mind from the time are Peter Bonetti (Chelsea) and Ron Springett (Sheffield Wednesday).

Full Backs that were stars of the day were:

Gerry Byrne (Liverpool)

George Cohen (Fulham)

Ray Wilson (Huddersfield)

Don Howe (WBA)

And Jimmy Armfield (Blackpool)

Jimmy joined Blackpool at the age of 17 on the 27th of December 1954.

He was part of the side that finished Runners Up in the First Division in the 1955-56 season.

Armfield was awarded the Young Player of the Year in 1959.

He made his international debut for England on 13th May 1959 against Brazil in front of 120,000 fans at the Maracana Stadium. He played in the 1962 World Cup in Chile.

Wing Halves that graced the pitch were:

Bobby Collins (Leeds United)

Ron Flowers (Wolverhampton W)

Bobby Moore (West Ham)

Danny Blanchflower (Tottenham)

Danny signed for Glentoran in 1946, then signed for Barnsley in 1949 for £6,000. He was later transferred to Aston Villa for £15,000.

In 1954, he made his move to Tottenham Hotspur for £30,000.

In the 1960-61 season, he was the captain that led the side to the First Division Title in the same season, Spurs completed the Double by beating Leicester City in the F.A. Cup Final.

Blanchflower was voted Football Writers Association Footballer of the Year in 1958 and again in 1961.

Spurs retained the F.A. Cup the following year against Burnley. He scored a penalty in a 3-1 victory.

In 1963, he captained the side to victory against Atletico Madrid in the European Cup Winners Cup Final.

He made his international debut for Northern Ireland in 1949 and captained the side in the 1958 World Cup Campaign as they reached the quarterfinals of the competition.

In 1962, he received his 50th cap for his country, the first Northern Irishman to achieve this.

Other Wing Halves included:

Billy Bremner (Leeds United)

Gordon Milne (Liverpool)

Dave Mackay (Tottenham)

Norman Hunter (Leeds United)

The big Centre Halves who were prominent were:

Maurice Norman (Tottenham)

Jackie Charlton (Leeds United)

Brian Labone (Everton)

Brian made his debut for Everton in 1958. He played in the First Division title winning team of 1962-63 season.

The flying wingers were:

Alan Ball (Blackpool)

Terry Paine (Southampton)

Martin Peters (West Ham)

John Connelly (Burnley)

Ian Callaghan (Liverpool)

Cliff Jones (Tottenham)

Bobby Charlton (Manchester Utd)

Bobby was born in Ashington, Northumberland. Making his debut for Manchester United at the age of 18 in 1956.

In the winning side of 1957 that took the Football League Division One Title playing as a winger with great speed and wonderful agility.

He was involved in the Munich Air Disaster of February 1958. He survived the crash to go on to win the 1963 F.A Cup with United.

Just two months after the Air Crash He made his debut for England in the April of 1958 against Scotland, scoring in that match in a 4 - 0 victory.

He was selected for the 58 World Cup Squad but didn't play in any of the matches.

Goal scoring Inside Forwards:

Ivor Allchurch (Cardiff)

George Eastman (Arsenal)

Denis Law (Manchester City)

Roger Hunt (Liverpool)

Jimmy Greaves (Tottenham)

Jimmy began his professional career with Chelsea in 1957. With 124 First Division goals in his first four seasons, he was sold to A.C. Milan for £80,000 in April 1961.

After a very short spell there, Tottenham paid £99,999 in December 1961 for his services.

He was in the 1961-62 F.A. Cup winning team and the 1962-63 winning European Cup Winners side.

He helped Spurs to a second place in the First Division in 1962-63.

Greaves won his first cap for England on 17th May 1959 against Peru.

He scored consecutive hat-tricks in October 1960 against both Northern Ireland and Luxembourg. He scored another hat-trick against Scotland in April 1961 in a 9-3 victory.

He played in all of the England 1962 World Cup matches.

On the 20th of November 1963, he scored four goals in an 8-3 win over Northern Ireland. Jimmy was a goal machine.

The men upfront through the middle were:

Geoff Hurst (West Ham)

Bobby Tambling (Chelsea)

Bobby Smith (Tottenham)

Sometimes I would switch their positions around, but not very often, as I always wanted to get things right and play the players in their proper spots.

I was also becoming aware of Foreign Footballers.

I remember finding an old diary in the back of a cupboard drawer, our drawers were always crowded, full with all sorts of items, some treasured and some that were there and forgotten about, there were always a pack of cards and pens in the drawers when needed.

Anyway, the diary hadn't been used, but it had photos in the back pages of World Football Stars of the Day:

Pele (Santos)

Raymond Kopa (Reims)

Ferenc Puskas (Real Madrid)

Josef Masopust (Dukla Prague)

Uwe Seeler (Hamburg)

Francisco Gento (Real Madrid)

Lev Yashin (Dynamo Moscow)

Eusebio (Benfica)

Djalma Santos (Palmeiros)

Karl Heinz Schnellinger (Roma)

Alfredo Di Stefano (Real Madrid)

It certainly helped me learn about places on the globe, as I would check out my Atlas for far-flung destinations in South America and Europe, what seemed like mystical places to me.

My 1964 XI

1
Gordon Banks
(Leicester City)

2
Jimmy Armfield
(Blackpool)

3
Ray Wilson
(Huddersfield Town)

4
Dave Mackay
(Tottenham Hotspur)

5
Maurice Norman
(Tottenham Hotspur)

6
Bobby Moore
(West Ham United)

7
Bobby Charlton
(Manchester United)

11
Cliff Jones
(Tottenham Hotspur)

8
Jimmy Greaves
(Tottenham Hotspur)

10
Denis Law
(Manchester United)

9
Bobby Smith
(Tottenham Hotspur)

Chapter 7: Cricketing Chess Match

News Headlines

In a thrilling showdown at Wembley, West Ham emerged victorious in the F.A. Cup Final by defeating Preston North End with a score of 3-2.

In South Vietnam, attacks by Communist Terrorists, the Vietcong, have some success sinking a U.S. transport ship and the ambush of government troops.

Plans launched by Lord Mayor of London raising a Million Pounds towards a National Memorial to President Kennedy. To set up a trust fund for British students to study at certain U.S. colleges and the erection of a Memorial Plinth at Runnymede. The students will be known as 'Kennedy Scholars'.

More than forty covert microphones have been found embedded in the walls of the American Embassy in Moscow, according to information released by the U.S. State Department.

Death of Jawaharial Nehru, the first Prime Minister of the Indian Union.

Total of 155 cases of typhoid were confirmed in Aberdeen. The most severe outbreak in the UK since 1937.

So here we are at Lords, the home of English Cricket, the tannoy is playing Roy Orbison's 'It's Over', but it was about to begin.

The sacred turf is green and gleaming, the crowd is anticipating a tremendous day of cricket. One innings to decide this year's Champions, it's either the Old Country England or Australia.

The teams are announced in the particular match, all the stars are on show; Ken Barrington, Bob Simpson, Geoff Boycott, Ted Dexter, Bill Lawry, McKenzie and Burge, and of course fiery Fred Trueman, plus many more.

Just before play begins, Chuck Berry comes over the airways with 'No Particular Place to Go'.

In fact, I am down on my knees in the sitting room. I can't use the front room as it is full of wallpaper. Paint, brushes and tables. There is always something going on in that front room.

A couple of months ago, it was out of bounds because it was chock-a-block with cardboard boxes. Inside were loads of Easter Eggs for the family. The smell was fantastic, and it was certainly a no-go area for kids.

Anyway, it's just me and my set of chess pieces. My sacred turf is a large green rug, a perfectly smooth surface to play this very special cricket match on.

Cricketers in question are the actual chessmen. The wicket is a small empty matchbox, and the ball is a screwed-up piece of silver paper from my Grandad's cigarette packet.

Eleven White Chess pieces take to the field.

The King, Queen, Knights, Rooks, Bishops and three Pawns. with a small circle of cardboard glued to the bottom of each piece, approximately ½" in diameter.

Everyone is numbered and represents an English player.

They are placed in fielding positions on the pitch.

Silly Mid-off, Silly Mid-on (Very silly short leg) far too dangerous even for a chess piece. Wicket Keeper, Third Man, Point, Fine Leg, (further back mighty fine leg), Mid-on, Long Off, Cover, Gully, Square Leg, many places and more.

This became the most complicated game, having seen my cousin Ian playing something similar. I tweaked it up and made it more technical and it was really hard to explain to others how it worked, so I didn't bother telling anyone and stayed in my imaginary world with the commentary voices of Alan Gibson and Robert Hudson.

Anyway, here I will try to explain. Not easy, but I will certainly give it a go.

The small silver ball is thrown gently by my right hand and in my left hand is a small lollipop stick made to look like a cricket bat.

I attempt to hit the ball. If I miss, and it hits the wicket, an appeal for a wicket takes place. This is where a die comes into play.

I throw the dice:

- 1 or 2 means the player is bowled out.
- 3 and the player is Stumped by the wicketkeeper.
- 4 means it is an LBW (Leg Before Wicket)
- 5 means Run Out
- 6 means Not Out, and 4 Extras given to the scorecard.

For a player to be caught out, the ball must rest within the small cardboard circle attached to the fielding Chessman.

To score runs where the ball lands after being hit by the lollipop bat, determines whether the batsman has scored 1 run, 2, 3, and obviously a 4 over the rope around the pitch, the rope (a piece of string), or 6 over the rope in the air.

To add to the realism, I write down every ball bowled on my scorepad. A process which is painfully slow and laborious, but to me only adds to the feeling of it being as close to a real game as I can get, which is very satisfying.

How the Final Scoreboard looked that day

	England (England wins by 5 runs)			
1.	G. Boycott	ct Simpson	b. Corling	52
2.	J. Edrich	ct Redparth	b. Simpson	67
3.	E. Dexter	ct Grout	b. Hawke	58
4.	C. Cowdrey		b. Hawke	40
5.	K. Barrington	LBW	b. McKenzie	116
6.	P. Parfitt		b. McKenzie	15
7.	J. Parks	ct Hawke	b. Vievers	50
8.	F. Titmus		b. Corling	29
9.	F. Trueman	ct Redpath	b. Hawke	8
10.	N. Gifford	ct Hawke	b. Corling	3
11.	L. Colwell	Not Out		1
	Extras			12
			Total	451

	Australia			
1.	W. Lawry		b. Trueman	86
2.	I. Redpath	ct Parfitt	b. Coldwell	76
3.	N. O'Neill	ct Titmus	b. Dexter	25
4.	P. Burge	LBW	b. Titmus	49
5.	B. Booth	st Parks	b. Titmus	20
6.	R. Simpson	ct Parfitt	b. Trueman	101
7.	T. Veivers	ct Parks	b. Coldwell	40
8.	G. McKenzie	ct Cowdrey	b. Trueman	4
9.	N. Hawke	Not Out		14
10.	A. Grout		b. Gifford	15
11.	G. Corling		b. Trueman	0
	Extras			16
			Total	446

Chapter 8: Thrills and Spills on the Imaginary Turf

News Headlines

At 50 years old, Scobie Breasley, last year's top jockey, secures his first Derby victory riding Santa Claus.

20th Anniversary of D-Day celebrated by reunion of representatives of Allied forces on sites of Normandy landings.

It is announced that West Germany will pay £1 Million in compensation to British victims of Nazi persecution.

Birth of a daughter to the World's First Space Woman, Nikolayeva Tereshkova.

In the Radfan Mountain area, federal troops from Aden, British and Saudi Arabia have taken control of what is thought to be the last rebel stronghold.

In South Australia, The Beatles arrived with the exception of Ringo, who was unable to join them due to illness. Despite his absence, the band was greeted by enthusiastic crowds in Adelaide.

Eight men in South Africa have been sentenced to life imprisonment for sabotage and conspiracy against the Government. Among those included was Nelson Mandela, famously known as the 'Black Pimpernel'. The sentences have caused worldwide indignation and demonstrations of protest.

Typhoid cases in Aberdeen rise to almost 400, it has reached its peak.

Senator Edward Kennedy, youngest brother of the late U.S. President, is injured in a Massachusetts Plane Crash.

Leyland Motors contract to supply Cuba 500 more buses, taking the total to 950 with a value of £9 Million.

Queen Elizabeth visits Aberdeen as the city reopens to visitors after overcoming the epidemic.

5th Race

French Grand Prix Result

Place	Driver	Car
1	Clark	Lotus
2	Maggs	Jaguar Fire Chief Van
3	G. Hill	BRM
4	Mitter	Ford Zephyr Police Car
5	McLaren	Ford Consul Cortina
6	Hailwood	Riley Pathfinder
7	Taylor	Mister Softee Ice-Cream Van
8	Amon	Hillman Imp
9	Ireland	Rolls Royce Silver Wraith
10	Anderson	Austin Seven
11	Brabham	Aston Martin DB4
12	Bandini	Ford Anglia
13	Gurney	Alfa Romeo
14	Siffert	Citroen DS19
15	Spence	Bedford AA Road Services Van

Retired from Race	
Driver	Car
P. Hill	Sheriffs Oldsmobile
Bonnier	Fiat
Surtees	Shark Nose Ferrari
Ginther	Vanwall
Arundell	RAF Vanguard Staff Car

Driver Standings after 5 Races

Place	Driver	Car	Points
1st	Clark	Lotus	28
2nd	Ginther	Vanwall	17
3rd	Brabham	Aston Martin DB4	13
	Surtees	Shark Nose Ferrari	13
5th	G. Hill	BRM	7
6th	Amon	Hillman Imp	6
	Gurney	Alfa Romeo	6
	Maggs	Jaguar Fire Chief Van	6
9th	Ireland	Rolls Royce Silver Wraith	5
10th	Bandini	Ford Anglia	4
11th	Arundell	RAF Vanguard Staff Car	3
	Mitter	Ford Zephyr Police Car	3
	Hailwood	Riley Pathfinder	3
14th	P. Hill	Sheriffs Oldsmobile	2
	Mclaren	Ford Consul Cortina	2
16th	Siffert	Citroen DS19	1
	Spence	Bedford AA Road Services Van	1

It was Saturday night, 'Family Night', the tea had been eaten, the washing up finished, and the kitchen was in a tidy order.

Yes, it was Escalado time. The radio was playing Dusty Springfield's 'Just Don't Know What to Do with Myself' and next on was Barron Knights 'Call Up the Bands'.

The News Headlines

Roy Emerson from Australia won the Men's Singles title at Wimbledon.

Maria Bueno achieved an impressive third victory in the Ladies' title, demonstrating her exceptional skill and competitive prowess on the tennis court.

Nyasaland becomes the Independent Commonwealth Republic of Malawi.

Donald Campbell shattered the World Car Speed record, reaching an astounding 403.1 mph.

In South Vietnam, the town of Cai Be, located 53 kilometres southwest of Saigon, has been seized by Communist guerrilla forces of the Viet Cong.

The news is interrupted by the sounds of the Beatles 'Hard Day's Night'. It's great listening to the music, as I am now setting up the Horse Racing game.

News Headlines Continued

John White, a Tottenham, and Scottish international footballer was killed by a lightning strike.

The Union of Post Office Workers is calling for nationwide strikes involving postmen and sorters.

Violent racial riots by night in Brooklyn, New York.

The House of Commons passes all party motion, paying tribute to Sir Winston Churchill, who is about to retire from the house.

Ranger 7 spacecraft lands on the Moon, after successfully televising pictures during the final 13 minutes.

Cricket match, 4th England v Australia Test ends in a draw at Old Trafford as each side scored over 600 runs in their first innings, leaving no time for further play.

The music drifts away in the air, the Rolling Stones 'It's All Over Now', followed by the Animals 'House of The Rising Sun'.

I turned off the radio and stretched the Green Blaze Cloth, with its little wooden blocks placed along the racetrack to hinder the Horses. Brackets are screwed onto the kitchen table to keep it in place.

The brightly coloured horses and jockeys are parading on the draining board next to the sink.

I had already created the Racecard for the night's entertainment.

Eleven races were about to commence.

My Mum and Nan would get involved as spectators and a little bit of gambling would be involved as both my Grandad and Dad enjoyed a flutter, and they would join the group.

A phrase that was always said about picking the winner, 'You couldn't tip Rubbish', mainly used by my Grandad, the joke of the evening was 'Is there a horse running called 'Dusty Carpet', it can't be beat'.

My Dad really did like a bet, but always within his means. He would bet on two flies on a wall to see which one would fly off first. I do remember my favourite saying, 'Two raindrops running down a window in the rain', betting on which would reach the bottom first.

The colourful metal horses with their jockeys on board were put into the starting position and, like everything I did, names would always have to be given.

This time to the Jockeys, not so much the horses.

The horses would be named in the final race of the night, a Special Champions Race.

    In   Blue was Scobie Breasley

             Green was Eddie Hide

             Red was Lester Piggott

             White was Yves Saint Martin

    and   Yellow was Jimmy Lindley

The scene for the first race was at the Happy Valley Racecourse, for the Hong Kong Classic.

Anticipation for the race to begin as all eyes are focused on the green track.

I am frantically turning the handle on the contraption that drives the horses and jockeys forward.

The riders and their mounts jostle for position, some getting knocked by the little wooden blocks, but coming through on the outside is Scobie Breasley on the blue horse for the first win of the evening.

Bets are being settled, pennies are changing hands, as I prepare for the Kentucky Derby at Churchill Downs.

The rest of the card includes trips to Ascot for the Gold Cup, over to France for the Prix L'Arc De Triomphe at Longchamp.

Two classics, The Oaks, and the Derby at Epsom.

I try to do a running commentary on the Derby race as if I am Peter O'Sullivan with my best mimicking voice.

We then go to the Irish Derby at the Curragh, followed by Doncaster's St. Ledger.

The last two races before the final special race of the night are the 1,000 and 2,000 Guineas at Newmarket.

The evening ends with a trip to Nottingham for the Ford Flat Race for Champions.

The horses and jockeys line up for the final time.

Beasley on Santa Claus

Hide on Cantelo

Piggott on St. Paddy

Yves Saint Martin on Relko

Lindley on Only for Life

Final bets are on.

"And they are OFF"

Cantelo takes an early lead, Reckoner comes up on the outside to challenge at the halfway mark.

Santa Claus and St. Paddy start to make their move, Only For Life is trailing in last place and making no headway, as they come to the final furlong it's a tight battle between Beasley and Piggott, but it's Piggott on St. Paddy that takes the crown by a head, 2nd place goes to Santa Claus, 3rd to Relko, 4th to Cantelo, with last place going to Only For Life.

1st   Piggott

2nd   Beasley

3rd   Saint Martin

4th   Hide

5th   Lindley

Chapter 9: Childhood Battles

It was around the time my Dad was posted abroad to Bahrain for a year, unaccompanied.

So, my Mum, sister Melanie and I moved in with my Mum's parents.

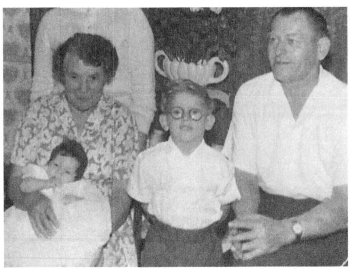

Me and my sister with my Mum's Parents: Daisy and Frank Thorpe

A nice house in the village of Digby, which was only 6 miles from my birthplace of Sleaford, Lincolnshire with the Beck running through the village and the Church dedicated to St. Thomas A Becket. This is where my Mum and Dad were married, it is a picturesque place.

What an impressive building the Church is, with architecture from many periods including Saxon sitting in the middle of the village with its tall spire which was struck by lightning in 1907 and cost £80 to repair.

There was also a Circular Stone Lock Up which in past times was used to keep drunks and troublemakers locked up for a time.

Then there was the local shop where I used to get my sweets from Mrs Flo Tasker, and of course there was the Primary School, oh no another school for me to go to and new people to meet big and small, here we go again.

It was hard to see Dad going away for such a long time, but I had to turn this into another adventure.

My older cousins lived in the same village, so I would see a lot more of them, and we always got on well together.

Yes, one big drawback would be another school to attend and that new boy situation I always found myself in and having to fit in once more.

Everything had become an adventure in my mind, even bath time took on a new meaning. I wasn't just a case of running the water and having a good soak.

How I ever linked Toy Soldiers, Wrestling, and having a bath, certainly proved to me how vivid my imagination was.

For the bath-time was never a normal affair.

I would put the plug in and slowly run the taps and arrange my toy soldiers in the bottom of the bath. All stood up.

These soldiers were large, about 5 inches tall.

There were eight of them, all in a variety of colours and poses. Two dark green ones were American World War 2 soldiers.

I called the first one Bert Royle. He held a rifle in his right hand and appeared to be moving forward. The second one was Vic Faulkner. He stood with his rifle shoulder high, aiming with the butt of the gun.

There were three in a sandy brown colour, and they were Japanese.

Number one was Billy Two Rivers, a soldier pointing to the right with his binoculars in his left hand.

Number two was Kendo Nagasaki, charging forward with a pained expression, a knife, and a revolver in each hand.

Number three was called Les Kellet. He had a large sword in his right hand, raised above his head.

84

And finally, three Germans. One standing with his arms wide, hand grenade in hand, leg astride, with another grenade tucked into his belt. His name was Jackie Pallo.

The second, a rifleman, taking aim and moving forward, is known as Steve Logan.

The third, his arm raised with his gun hanging over his shoulder, he was Mick McManus.

Of course, these were all well-known Television Wrestlers seen on the screen, Wednesdays, and Saturdays.

Simply, the game I played was to see which soldier/fighter was to wobble and topple into the water. The last man standing was the winner.

Then it was proper bath time for me with plenty of bubbles.

As I got in, the toys would float around me as I used to dive bomb them off the side of the bath.

We had a metal basket/tidy thing which stretched across, which we kept the flannel, sponge, and soap in. It became a springboard for the wrestlers as I made them tumble and spin into the soapy water.

I would even give them a score for each dive.

I also had an old plastic pirate ship. It had taken quite a battering and consisted of just the hull section.

The sails and deck had been destroyed long ago, but this was perfect to carry the soldiers in as they floated around the sea/bath water.

When I was out of the bath, I spent many hours play-fighting with these characters, two falls, a submission, or a knockout to decide their fate.

In real life, Billy Two Rivers was a Canadian Mohawk, complete with a Mohaecan hairstyle and feathered headdress and a celebrity War Dance.

Kendo, the real name Peter Thornley, was always portrayed as a Samurai, with the supposed ability to hypnotise.

I teamed these two together as a tag team.

Royle and Faulkner became the Fabulous Royle Brothers. Bert's special move was the flying head kick.

Pallo, with his pig-tail bleached hair, stood in his striped shorts.

Kellet, who always appeared punch drunk, looking defeated in his fight before coming back from the brink.

Bryle-creamed slick black-haired Steve Logan known as Iron Man, a real tough guy in the ring was paired with the one the fans loved to boo at every opportunity, Mick McManus, whose specialty was his short-range forearm jab.

My Grandad used to watch Wrestling on Television, Wednesday nights and Saturday afternoons. I used to watch it with him, but I had to be very quiet. I don't know why because it was a noisy affair, especially as he used to shout and curse at the telly. You could hardly hear Kent Walton's commentary as Grandad would boo McManus every move around the ring.

These were special times with him. I can see his stained nicotine fingers quite yellow from many years smoking Woodbines and strong Navy cigarettes.

He would occasionally tell me a ghost story. One tale that has stayed with me was about how Digby Churchyard was haunted in the 1930's. A young dark haired man who lived in the village had been in the public house, and was walking home through the Churchyard, he was a little worse for wear and was tired so he settled down resting against one of the carved gravestones.

He was hungry and remembered he had an apple in his pocket, he reached into his other pocket and felt for his pen knife. He took it out and was going to cut into the apple, when suddenly he felt something tugging at his coat, he turned his face to look behind him, there was nothing there, he went to cut the fruit again, he felt something touching him and the same tugging of his coat sleeve. Once more warily he turned, but again there was nothing there, just darkness he was now so scared he passed out.

The next morning, he was found lying on the ground by the local Vicar. He helped the man to his feet; the man's hair had turned from jet black to white overnight. The Vicar noticed the man's pen knife was caught by one of the extra blades in the sleeve of his coat.

With that Grandad said, "Sleep well lad, I will see you in the morning."

News Headlines

In the Gulf of Tonkin, a U.S. destroyer was targeted by three North Vietnamese torpedo boats, leading to an attack.

50th Anniversary of Great Britain's declaration of war against Germany in the First World War.

Four Turkish aircraft conducted an attack on ports located in Northwest Cyprus. Subsequently, Greek Cypriot forces retaliated by launching attacks on Turkish Cypriot villages.

Charles Frederick Wilson sentenced to 30 years' imprisonment for his leading part in the Great Train Robbery escapes from a Birmingham jail.

In the final cricket match at the Oval this year, England v Australia. F.S. Trueman, Yorkshire bowler, has taken his 300th Wicket in Test Cricket.

The International Olympic Committee has decided to prohibit all South African participation in the 18th Olympic Games.

The sounds of Manfred Man's 'Do Wah Diddy Diddy' play through the airwaves, followed by the Honeycombes 'Have I The Right'.

6th Race

Belgium Grand Prix Result

Place	Driver	Car	Points
1	McLaren	Ford Consul Cortina	8
2	Gurney	Alfa Romeo	6
3	Bonnier	Fiat	4
4	Arundell	RAF Vanguard Staff Car	3
5	Mitter	Ford Zephyr Police Car	2
6	Bandini	Ford Anglia	1
7	Ginther	Vanwall	
8	Clark	Lotus	
9	Hailwood	Riley Pathfinder	
10	Spence	Bedford AA Road Services Van	
11	Anderson	Austin Seven	

Retired from Race	
Driver	**Car**
Maggs	Jaguar Fire Chief Van
Surtees	Shark Nose Ferrari
P. Hill	Sheriffs Oldsmobile
Siffert	Citroen DS19
G. Hill	BRM
Brabham	Aston Martin DB4
Amon	Hillman Imp
Ireland	Rolls Royce Silver Wraith
Taylor	Mister Softee Ice-Cream Van

Driver Standing after 6 Races

Place	Driver	Car	Points
1st	Clark	Lotus	28
2nd	Ginther	Vanwall	17
3rd	Brabham	Aston Martin DB4	13
	Surtees	Shark Nose Ferrari	13
5th	Gurney	Alfa Romeo	12
6th	McLaren	Ford Consul Cortina	10
7th	G. Hill	BRM	7
8th	Amon	Hillman Imp	6
	Maggs	Jaguar Fire Chief Van	6
	Arundell	RAF Vanguard	6
11th	Bandini	Ford Anglia	5
	Ireland	Rolls Royce Silver Wraith	5
	Mitter	Ford Zephyr Police Car	5
14th	Bonnier	Fiat	4
15th	Hailwood	Riley Pathfinder	3
16th	P. Hill	Sheriffs Oldsmobile	2
17th	Siffert	Citroen DS19	1
	Spence	Bedford AA Road Services Van	1

I settled in my new school in Digby, and all was well until I had a run-in with the local lads and one particular boy, the leader of the gang, which consisted of only three other boys. Pop Roberts was his name why Pop I didn't really know but I knew he was a bully. He didn't like the idea of a R.A.F. a boy in his school thought it was just for villagers, not outsiders.

On the way home a couple of times, I was ambushed by the gang, but I was quick on my feet and managed to run away from them. On the third occasion, I was not so lucky. Suddenly surrounded by the four boys, with nowhere to run, this time it was time to fight. I chose to stand my ground and challenge Pop, to be fair the other three boys stood back and let us take each other on, there were no punches thrown but a lot of grabbing and pulling as we both ended up on the ground neither really gaining a real grip of each other.

From around the corner, a man appeared. He lifted us both up and, as he did, our heads banged together. Whether we did that, or he did, I don't know. But I do know that the fighting stopped. We were made to shake hands and from that moment; I was left alone by the gang.

We were never friends, but I was never bullied again by Pop Roberts or anyone else in the village. I had earned my stripes.

Chapter 10: Cowboy Town Confrontation

I could hear my Nan in the kitchen cooking and singing along to the radio. I was amazed she knew the words to the Four Seasons 'Rag Doll'. In addition, I could hear my Mum joining in with 'You Really Got Me', a hit for the Kinks, and then 'I'm Into Something Good' by Herman's Hermits.

I knew my Nan would be wearing her pinafore apron. On the stove would be cabbage boiling away, the smell wafting through the air.

News Headlines

British, New Zealand, and Gurkha troops have been deployed to provide support to Malaysian forces in repelling Indonesian invaders.

The Queen opens the new road bridge over the Forth, at present the largest suspension bridge in Europe.

R.A.F. fighters attack Indonesian guerilla positions in the Malaya jungle.

There has been yet another military coup in South Vietnam.

Last issue of the Daily Herald Labour Party newspaper founded in 1912.

The scheduled date for the British election has been announced as October 15th.

The New British national newspaper 'The Sun' replaces the 'Daily Herald' under the same editorship and using the same presses.

Malta achieves independence.

The passing of Harpo Marx, a prominent member of the renowned Marx Brothers, has occurred in Hollywood.

Picture the scene, a Cowboy Town is on the hallway floor. It could be a scene from a Western film set, any of the Hollywood Movies of the day.

The 7th Cavalry with its Fort Abraham Lincoln or perhaps one of the films about the many tribes of Indians, The Searchers, Comanches, Run of the Arrow with the Sioux, also Mexicans at the Alamo.

The town is situated just by the large Rubber Plant in its big heavy red pot, the striped curtains two shades of brown hanging from the rail above the front door. They are partly pulled together to block out the midday sun, which was shining down on what appeared to be a peaceful setting.

There was the General Store, The Bank (Nathaniel West), Saloon with its impressive swinging doors, The Livery Stables, Blacksmiths, and of course the Sheriff's Office with the dreaded jail at the back.

The Cowboys were placed around the town, along with Cavalry soldiers and Mexicans, and some of these given names.

I always had an array of characters, famous film stars of the day.

Rod Steiger, Burt Lancaster, Randolph Scott, Yul Bryner, Henry Fonda, Jimmy Stewart, and Walter Brennan.

A scouting party consisting of Gill Favor, Rowdy Yates, and Bronco Lane, led by Clayton Moore and Jay Silverheels and, of course, the hero Glenn Ford. These were portrayed by the little toy figures.

I could always pick out which one was which as I made a running commentary of the action. As if I was the Great Director of my own picture in real life Technicolour.

All the Great Chiefs are assembled with their men:

The Apache with Cochise, Crazy Horse, Geronimo, and Little Raven.

The Navajo with Manuelito.

The Cheyenne with Morning Star.

The Comanche with Quanah Parker.

And the Sioux with Red Cloud and Sitting Bull.

A very remarkable sight as all the tribes join together on horseback a little away back from the action, waiting for the right moment to attack.

The rest of the Tribes are in the Mountains high above.

Actually, it's the Stairs looking down on what would become a besieged town. They were primed and ready for the fight to begin.

I would carefully climb the stairs, unlike my Grandad going up to the bathroom.

Standing on my Indians willy nilly, as they fall to their untimely deaths, as he makes his way on his vital journey.

As I traverse this mountain range, I would carry a supply of elastic bands and a 12" rule.

A round of six shots rained down on the Town.

The band stretched the full length of the rule, aimed, and released at the hapless unexpected targets.

The elastic band hitting the plastic figures, knocking them down to their demise; some were very lucky and were spun around to fall back to fall against a building or totter and staying upright, to fall to the ground would indicate a fatal shot.

The dead bodies would be removed from the scene.

Tip-toeing carefully, making my way down the treacherous mountains to resume the reply from the Township.

As they looked up at the enemy, they would fire back. Again, I would take aim with another round of six elastic band shots.

In turn, this action would carry on. After a short while, the Indians on horseback would enter the arena.

As the Townsfolk started to panic, the Cavalry would spring into action, trumpets blowing and flags flying.

An oversized wagon with a large white billowing canopy and a large Red Stagecoach driven by two white horses appears.

As they are filled with people, it makes its way further back into the hallway to a Wooden Fort for refuge.

Fort Laramie was their last hope of survival.

The fighting continues throughout the day, until the Town is ransacked, and the Fort destroyed, or the Indians retreat to fight another day, or they fight to the very bitter end and are defeated on the battlefield.

The Scenario changes each time I play. Sometimes the Indians win and other times the Townsfolk would fight gallantly with the Cavalry and win the day.

A hard-fought battle, John Ford, the man of Legend in the Film World, would be proud of all the Cinematic Splendour.

Chapter 11: The Iconic Streets of Monaco

Grand Prix 7th Race

Monaco Grand Prix

All was set on a glorious sunny day for what was to be undoubtedly an exciting race.

The engines were running and when the flag fell, all the cars got away to a perfect start.

The two leaders, Gurney in the Alfa Romeo, and Maggs in the Jaguar Fire Chief led up the hill to the Casino, a well-placed Fruit Bowl full of Oranges and Apples.

The two of them were still in command at the end of the opening lap.

The order was: Gurney, Maggs, Graham Hill, Clark, Surtees, and McLaren.

The first nine cars were nose to tail.

A quarter of the way through the race, Clark in 2nd was desperately trying to get past the leader: Surtees. In spite of this furious battle for the lead, the majority of the field was keeping up.

Close by, Ginther, McLaren, Ireland, G. Hill, Maggs and Gurney, all one behind each other.

Trouble had already struck the field as Siffert's Citroen, Phil Hill's Oldsmobile and Bandini's Ford Anglia had all withdrawn from the proceedings.

Behind the front eight were Taylor in his distinctive Ice-Cream Van, Bonnier in the Fiat, Brabham's Yellow Aston Martin, Spence in the AA Service van, with Anderson's small Red Austin 7.

They were all spread out and running what appeared a separate race.

By the halfway mark, Amon had left the race with transmission failure to his Hillman Imp.

Mitter in the Ford Zephyr, Arundel in his RAF Vanguard and Hailwood travelling in the Riley Pathfinder were trailing way behind the rest of the field.

Now with three quarters of the race behind them, Brabham overtook Gurney and moved into seventh place. Innis Ireland sat in the Silver Wraith Rolls Royce and was placed 6th but running into trouble with gearbox problems and had to pull out of the race.

There was no letting up among the first five.

McLaren leading, Clark in 2nd, Graham Hill in 3rd, Surtees in 4th and Ginther in 5th.

So, it was the Ford Consul, Cortina, Lotus, BRM, Ferrari and Vanwall flashing by.

Eventually Gurney coasted his Alfa Romeo into the pits to retire with a broken crown wheel and pinion.

In the final 10 laps, Clark had slipped out of the pack and was battling with Brabham for 5th position.

Graham Hill and Ginther had pulled away in the front, McLaren decided to settle for the 3rd place and dropped back from the leading two.

Surtees declared his intentions and had one final go at winning the battle.

He couldn't get past McLaren and had to settle for 4th position.

The BRM and Vanwall romped home with Hill just edging Ginther to the finishing line.

7th Race

Monaco Grand Prix Result

Place	Driver	Car
1	G. Hill	BRM
2	Ginther	Vanwall
3	McLaren	Ford Consul Cortina
4	Surtees	Shark Nose Ferrari
5	Brabham	Aston Martin DB4
6	Clark	Lotus
7	Spence	Bedford AA Road Services Van
8	Anderson	Austin Seven
9	Maggs	Jaguar Fire Chief Van
10	Mitter	Ford Zephyr Police Car
11	Arundell	RAF Vanguard
12	Hailwood	Riley Pathfinder
13	Bonnier	Fiat
14	Taylor	Mister Softee Ice-Cream Van

Retired from Race	
Driver	**Car**
Ireland	Rolls Royce Silver Wraith
Gurney	Alfa Romeo
Siffert	Citroen DS19
Amon	Hillman Imp
P. Hill	Sheriffs Oldsmobile
Bandini	Ford Anglia

Driver Standing after 7 Races

(With one race left to go)

Place	Driver	Car	Points
1st	Clark	Lotus	29
2nd	Ginther	Vanwall	23
3rd	Surtees	Shark Nose Ferrari	16
4th	Brabham	Aston Martin DB4	15
	G. Hill	BRM	15
6th	McLaren	Ford Consul Cortina	14
7th	Gurney	Alfa Romeo	12
8th	Amon	Hillman Imp	6
	Maggs	Jaguar Fire Chief Van	6
	Arundell	RAF Vanguard Staff Car	6
11th	Bandini	Ford Anglia	5
	Ireland	Rolls Royce Silver Wraith	5
	Mitter	Ford Zephyr Police Car	5
14th	Bonnier	Fiat	4
15th	Hailwood	Riley Pathfinder	3
16th	P. Hill	Sheriffs Oldsmobile	2
17th	Siffert	Citroen DS19	1
	Spence	Bedford AA Road Services Van	1

News Headlines

57 people escape from East to West Berlin through a tunnel under the Berlin Wall.

The Japanese Emperor opened the Olympic Games in Tokyo.

Death of Eddie Cantor, a popular U.S. film comedian of the 1930s, aged 72.

A Russian spacecraft has successfully launched into space, carrying three crew members. Among them are an army doctor and a scientist, who holds the distinction of being the first civilian to venture into orbit. This marks a significant milestone in civilian space travel and highlights the collaborative efforts in advancing space exploration.

Mr Khruschev, aged 70, is relieved of his duties as first secretary of the Communist Party of USSR and Prime Minister and is succeeded in the former office by Leonid Breshnev and in the latter by Alexei Kosygin.

The U.S. songwriter Cole Porter passed away at the age of 71.

China explodes her first atomic bomb.

Final returns in the UK General Election give the Labour Party an overall majority of the 5 in the House of Commons.

In the transition of leadership, Harold Wilson assumed the role of Prime Minister, replacing Sir Alec Douglas-Home.

Herbert Hoover, the 31st President of the United States from 1929 to 1933, passed away at the age of 90.

Last Day of the 1964 British flat racing marks Lester Piggott as the Champion Jockey with 140 wins.

Chapter 12: Unforgettable Triumphs and Rock & Roll

I watched loads of the Tokyo Summer Olympics on the Television.

The Athletics was a favourite of mine and especially watching the Man in Black, New Zealander Peter Snell on the cinder track, with his two outstanding performances in the 800m and 1500m. He crushed his opponents and gained two Gold Medals.

The other outstanding performance was from the Ethiopian soldier Bikila Abebe, who repeated his win from 1960 Rome Olympics taking the Gold in the gruelling Marathon.

Britain was superbly represented by Mary Rand, who won the Long Jump Gold and her roommate at the Olympics Ann Packer, who took the 800m Gold.

Two men who shone brightly for Britain winning Gold Medals were Ken Matthews in the 20km walk and Lyn Davies with his 26ft 5ins Long Jump victory.

With commentary from David Coleman, Max Robertson, Peter West, and Frank Bough they always made everything thrilling and exciting.

One particular commentary I remember was by Harry Carpenter when Joe Frazier won a Gold Medal in the Heavyweight boxing, Joe competing with a broken thumb.

Today at the Olympics was shown on TV at 10:15, Alan Weeks' 3pm show, which would provide the outstanding moments from the previous day's events.

Later in the evening would be the Olympic Report by Cliff Michelmore.

The Wonderful Opening Music on the BBC 'Tokyo Melody' by Helmut Zacharias grabbed you in and was so memorable from the first time it was heard, the instrumental was hard to put in words, but it sounded like DA DA — DA-DA DAR DA DAR DAR DAR DAD DAD DAR, well something like that.

My cousins Val and Ian, Val a massive Rolling Stones fan, her bedroom decked out with magazine pictures of the band, you could hardly see a trace of the flowered wallpaper as every inch was covered, Mick Jagger being her particular favourite but pictures of Charlie Watts the drummer, Keith Richards, Brian Jones and Bill Wyman decorated the room.

Ian was a Beatles fan, which seemed the total opposite to Val. I also preferred the Beatles. John, George, Ringo, and Paul were brilliant.

They were both in the sitting room playing some new 45's on the Red Dansette Record Player. Not the Stones or the Beatles this time.

I joined in to listen to three big hits of the time, The Supremes 'Where did our love go', Roy Orbison's 'Oh Pretty Woman' and Sandy Shaw' 'Always Something There to Remind Me'.

Being with them listening to music, the hits of the day, always made me feel good. They were both teenagers and so much older than me, just made me feel a little more grown up.

I can recall going into Lincoln on the bus with Ian, my Auntie Joyce and my Mum for a special treat, a meal in the J. Lyons Corner House but my mind could be playing tricks with me; it could have been just a very large cafe.

Afterwards we did some shopping in the big Department Stores. As we walked along the streets Ian and I made a Harry Worth impression, Harry was a very well-known Television Comedian of the day.

It was an optical illusion trick, getting to the end of one of the large shop windows on the corner, raising one arm and one leg, the reflection gave the impression of us leaving the ground, well it seemed fun to us.

News Headlines break into the music on the radio, interrupting the Kinks 'All of the Day and All of the Night'.

Viet Cong guerrillas attack a U.S. air base near Saigon, South Vietnam.

U.S. elections resulted in a decisive victory for President Johnson, a Democrat, over Senator Barry Goldwater, a Republican.

A ceasefire in the Yemen civil war has been agreed upon by representatives of the Royalists and the Republicans.

First anniversary of President Kennedy's assassination was commemorated in the USA, as well as in the UK and other countries.

The 90th birthday of Sir Winston Churchill is acclaimed the world over.

The Music resumes with The Supremes 'Baby Love'.

Chapter 13: Sports Galore

I am watching the BBC's Grandstand Sports programme, presented by David Coleman. Many different sports are shown like: Rugby League, Swimming, Boxing, Snooker, Horse Racing, Ice Hockey and, of course, Football.

Results at 5, but for now I am fully involved in watching Motorcycling Scrambling. Like any sport, if you take an interest in the competitors, it becomes more enjoyable.

I had come to know a handful of Motorcyclists: Dave Bickers, Jeff Smith, Vic Eastwood, Andy Lee, John Banks, Chris Horsefield, and Arthur Lampkin, I am even becoming more knowledgeable on the riders motorcycles: Greeves, BSA, Matchless and Husqvarna.

Lampkin always looked like a man on a mission, he was my favourite. Then there was Jeff Smith, who at the age of 30, achieved the 500cc Motocross World Championship and was voted 1964 Motorcycle News' Man of the Year award.

I was particularly interested in this type of racing because my Mum's cousins, Mick and Den Humberstone, were involved in sidecar racing. They used to race at Cadwell Park, a motor racing circuit located 5 miles south of Louth in Lincolnshire. The number on their sidecar and motorcycle was 252. Funny enough I have always remembered that number, my Dad told me it was a R.A.F. Charge report number that documented an alleged offence, 'Jankers' or being put on a fizzer. Strange what stays with you but I remember loads of stuff he told me, he certainly was a man with loads of interesting facts and wisdom.

I used to just soak up television programmes. I would watch so many shows, not just children's stuff like Pinky and Perky, the singing Piglets. Pinky wore red clothes and Perky wore blue, but that was of little use to us watching black and white television. Pinky often wore a hat that helped. They would sing the Big Chart Hits of the time.

Captain Pugwash was a short-animated series, the seafaring hero Captain Pugwash the pirate who sailed the high seas in his ship called the Black Pig. There was the cabin boy called Tom, pirates Willy and Barnabas and Master Mate.

Cut Throat Jake was his mortal enemy. He was the Captain of the Flying Dustman. It was great fun to watch. Pugwash being the bravest buccaneer, but he was really quite a coward.

The Boss Cat Cartoon Show, this was about a New York alley cat who was always trying to find ways to make money, helped by his gang of friends: Benny the Ball, Brain, Spook, Fancy-Fancy and Choo Choo.

A beat cop, Officer Dibble, was always on the lookout for T.C.

The Telegoons were a comedy puppet show. The voices of the original Goons: Harry Secombe, Peter Sellers and Spike Milligan reprised their original voice roles.

Blue Peter with Chris Tate and Valerie Singleton, the children's entertainment programme, there were always lots of arts and craft items on the show, and they showed you how to make things from the bits and pieces around the house.

Crackerjack with Eamon Andrews, Leslie Crowther, and Peter Glaze with their competitive games with children in the studio, the cast would always perform a play which was always funny.

One of the games I remember well was Double or Drop, three children would be given a prize for a question answered correctly but were given a cabbage if they got it wrong, they were out if they dropped any item or if they received a third cabbage.

The winner would receive a toy from a basket and the other two children would get a Crackerjack propelling pencil, a much-envied prize.

Then there was Doctor Who, a science fiction show. The Doctor was portrayed by William Hartnell. His spaceship was called the Tardis, which on the outside looked like a British Police Box, but inside it was enormous. The most frightening enemy of the Doctor was the Daleks and at first sight it was hide your eyes behind a cushion time, scary creatures Daleks with their strange voices.

Later in the evening, I would watch the Lucy Show starring Lucille Ball, or the Arthur Haynes Show. Then there was Dave's Kingdom with Dave King.

Some great music programmes, Ready Steady Go with Keith Fordyce and Cathy McGowan, a live show allowing the artists to perform their latest songs.

Juke Box Jury with its panel of celebrities who were asked to judge the recent record releases. With a Hit or a Miss, in one show the Rolling Stones appeared as Jurors on the panel, the only time there had been more than four jurors on the programme.

Top of the Pops, a chart show hosted by Jimmy Savile and Alan Freeman, acts would mime to their hits. The last song on the show would always be the Number One, Top of the Hit Parade.

My favourite Western shows were Wagon Train, Laramie, and Rawhide.

Wagon Train was an adventure story of a westbound wagon train from Missouri to California, right through the American frontier.

Laramie was mainly about two brothers, the Shermans - Slim and Andy and a drifter called Jess Harper, who became partners in the Sherman Ranch and Stagecoach Relay Station in Wyoming. It captured my imagination of what life was like to be a cowboy at that time.

Rawhide was my top watch when it came to Westerns. Just the names alone stirred up romantic illusions of the Wild West. Gil Favor, Rowdy Yates, Wishbone Haggerty, what wonderful names. It was set in the 1860s and was mainly about the Cattle Drive, some nearby town where there was always trouble. It was a lawless society.

Chapter 14: Golden Age of Television

In the evenings, I used to watch television with my family. The favourites in our household were:

The Saint with Roger Moore as Simon Templar. A charming and handsome gentleman/conman/playboy who was wanted by the Police. What was always fun to watch was the way Moore talked directly to the audience in the show.

No Hiding Place featuring Tom Lockheart as Detective Chief Superintendent, with tales of Scotland Yard.

Emergency Ward 10, a medical soap opera at a hospital called Oxbridge General.

Coronation Street was a must. With Ena Sharples, Minnie Caldwell, Albert Tatlock, Elsie Tanner and Len Fairclough giving us a feel for what appeared in the grimy North.

Dr Kildare, a medical drama starring Richard Chamberlain, who played the title role. It was set at 'Blair General Hospital.' He was always trying to gain the respect of his senior, Dr Leonard Gillespie.

Dixon of Dock Green with Jack Warner delivering the opening and closing lines of every episode, 'Evening All and Goodnight, all' as he stood outside the Police Station.

Z Cars set in New Town, a place in Northern England. The main characters were Fancy Smith, Bert Lynch, PC Jock Weir and Det. Sgt. Watt and Det. Chief Inspector Barlow.

These programmes gave me an insight into real life or life as it was portrayed on television and to a young mind had a profound effect on me in a good way, hopefully.

Two shows that come to mind are Game Shows, the first being Take Your Pick with Michael Miles, the bit I always enjoyed was the Yes/No Interlude, contestants would answer questions with 60 seconds on the clock, without using the word Yes or No. If they did, they would get gonged off the stage by Alec Dane, he was the man with the gong. But if they didn't say yes or no, they could Take the Money or Open the Box. To open the box, they picked a key, and one box included a special key to Box 13, which may have contained a really good prize like a holiday, but it could also contain a booby prize that was basically the choice, Win or Lose.

The rival game show was hosted by Hughie Green, and this was called Double Your Money. The prize money doubled from £1 to a guaranteed £32. If the contestant got that far, they would go into a Soundproof Booth to try to win more money, 2 correct answers for £64, 3 parts for £128, then it doubled again if they got 4 parts correct, eventually reaching a six-part question for the top prize of £1000 on the Treasure Trail.

Probably my favourite show on television was Steptoe and Son and one particular episode I remember was Sunday for Seven Days. Harold regrets taking Albert to the cinema. They are split over which film to see, Harold wants to see Felini's 8 1/2, in Harold's opinion a high brow film. While Albert prefers Nudes of 1964.

They go to see Felini's film. Albert settles and causes upset in the cinema and drags Harold inadvertently into an argument. They eventually get thrown out. The pair of them fallout, as Harold tells his Dad to go and see the film he originally wanted to see, upset Albert buys a ticket for one to see Nudes of 1964, which leaves Harold out in the cold. The final scene sees Harold change his mind and reluctantly goes into the cinema asking the Ticket Lady, where his Dad is sitting. He chose a seat as far as possible away from him.

The two entertainment shows I grew up with were Billy Cotton Band Show with Billy's call out 'Wakey Wakeeeeeeey!'. This was more introduction to piano music with Mrs Mills and Russ Conway.

Then there was the Black and White Minstrels Show, George Mitchell's Minstrels with principal singers Dai Francis, Tony Mercer, and John Boulter, singing lots of nostalgic medleys. Songs I used to sing along with were: Dixie, Oh Susanna, When the Saints Go Marching In were favourites of mine.

Other songs from an earlier era I knew word for word were: Me and My Shadow, Sitting on Top of the World and Carolina in the Morning.

My cousin Ian and I would often perform in front of the family, pretending to be Morecombe and Wise, singing Me and My Shadow. I used to put my hand on Ian's shoulder, and we would walk around the house in tune.

One of the Biggest Shows on television was the Royal Variety Show. The 1964 version was hosted by Jimmy Tarbuck, a young comedian star from Liverpool whose wit and humour captivated the audience, some of them seeing him for the first time. The stars and acts were:

Cilla Black (Singer) making her debut at the Royal Variety.

Morecambe and Wise (Comedians)

Gracie Fields (Singer)

Gil Dova (Juggling Act)

Moiseyev Dance Company (Ballet Troupe)

Bob Newhart (Comedian)

The Bachelors (Irish Singing Trio)

The Tiller Girls (Dance Troupe)

Dennis Spicer (Ventriloquist)

Millicent Martin (Singer and Comedian)

Kathy Kirby (Singer)

Brenda Lee (Singer)

Ralph Reader & the Gang Show

Lena Horne (Singer) with the Chico Hamilton Quartette

Cliff Richard & The Shadows (Singer & Group)

Tommy Cooper (Comedian and Magician)

And David Jacobs was introducing some of the acts.

Chapter 15: A Year of Cinematic Wonder

Final Race of the Grand Prix Season

8th Race

British Grand Prix

It was a fine start and after the oil and rubber had cleared, Brabham in the Aston Martin and Gurney in the Alfa Romeo were neck and neck in the first two places.

Concentrating hard in third was McLaren with his Ford Consul, just behind in fourth place sat Graham Hill's BRM with Clark sitting comfortably in the Lotus in fifth position.

Soon Clark moved through the field to not only take the lead, but he was very clear in front.

A quarter of the way through the race, it had split itself into three factions.

Clark was still drawing away with McLaren, Hill and Surtees driving his Ferrari chasing hard for second place.

The following group consisted of Taylor inside the Ice-Cream Van, Bonnier in the Fiat, Ireland's Rolls Royce, Ginther in the Vanwall, Bandini travelling smoothly with the Ford Anglia and Amon's Hillman Imp very close to the group. This created a very interesting battle.

The third group was being led by Anderson in the Austin Seven.

At the halfway point, the casualties were McLaren, Ireland and Taylor with his electric fuel pump not working properly.

Clark had an impressive lead over Brabham, Gurney, G. Hill, and Surtees. These had pulled clear of Bonnier, Ginther, Bandini and Amon.

The rest of the field at this point consisted of a colourful group of cars, Anderson's Austin Seven, Siffert's Citroen, Hailwood's Riley, Arundel's RAF Vanguard, Phil Hill's Sheriff's Oldsmobile, Mitter's Ford Zephyr Police Car, with Maggs in the Jaguar Fire Chief Van and Spence's Bedford Van.

By the three-quarter stage, it was clear no one was going to catch Jim Clark. Gurney had moved into 2nd place.

Spence, Siffert, and Bonnier had entered the pits and did not return to the race.

Third place now belonged to Graham Hill with John Surtees, Bandini, Ginther and Jack Brabham following.

Suddenly Gurney noticed all his oil pressure disappear, and he pulled off the circuit and was out of the race along with a sadly limping Aston Martin of Jack Brabham.

With the end in sight, Clark, comfortably ahead of Hill, slowed a little to make sure of the win even so he was a long way clear of his rivals.

Clark took the chequered flag. The excitement was now for second place, as Surtees rapidly gained on Hill and passed him to snatch the second spot, pushing Hill back into third. Bandini came in 4th with Ginther close behind on 5th.

Meanwhile, victorious World Champion Jim Clark was serenaded by a Scottish soldier playing Scotland the Brave on the bagpipes.

8th Race

British Grand Prix Result

Place	Driver	Car
1	Clark	Lotus
2	Surtees	Shark Nose Ferrari
3	G. Hill	BRM
4	Bandini	Ford Anglia
5	Ginther	Vanwall
6	Arundell	RAF Vanguard Staff Car
7	Anderson	Austin Seven
8	Maggs	Jaguar Fire Chief Van
9	Amon	Hillman Imp
10	P. Hill	Sheriffs Oldsmobile
11	Hailwood	Riley Pathfinder
12	Mitter	Ford Zephyr Police Car

Retired from Race	
Driver	**Car**
McLaren	Ford Consul Cortina
Ireland	Rolls Royce Silver Wraith
Taylor	Mister Softee Ice-Cream Van
Spence	Bedford AA Road Services Van
Siffert	Citroen DS19
Bonnier	Fiat
Gurney	Alfa Romeo
Brabham	Aston Martin DB4

Final Drivers Standing

Place	Driver	Car	Points
1st	Clark	Lotus	37
2nd	Ginther	Vanwall	25
3rd	Surtees	Shark Nose Ferrari	22
4th	G. Hill	BRM	19
5th	Brabham	Aston Martin DB4	15
6th	McLaren	Ford Consul Cortina	14
7th	Gurney	Alfa Romeo	12
8th	Bandini	Ford Anglia	8
9th	Arundell	RAF Vanguard Staff Car	7
10th	Amon	Hillman Imp	6
	Maggs	Jaguar Fire Chief Van	6
12tth	Ireland	Rolls Royce Silver Wraith	5
	Mitter	Ford Zephyr Police Car	5
14th	Bonnier	Fiat	4
15th	Hailwood	Riley Pathfinder	3
16th	P. Hill	Sheriffs Oldsmobile	2
17th	Spence	Bedford AA Road Services Van	1
	Siffert	Citroen DS19	1
	Taylor	Mister Softee Ice-Cream Van	0
	Anderson	Austin Seven	0

My Mum loved the pictures, and I was looking at a list of films I had seen at the cinema with her in the last 12 months.

22 Jan: ZULU

Starring Stanley Baker as John Chard and Michael Caine as Gonville Bromhead.

The Historic Battle of Rorke's Drift between the British Army 24th Regiment of Foot and the Zulu tribesmen. Whether it really happened or not in real life, the British soldiers singing 'Men of Harlech' back to the Zulu war chants remains a great memory from the film.

29th Jan: Dr Strangelove

Starring Peter Sellers playing 3 of the main parts.

2nd July: Wonderful Life

With Cliff Richard and the Shadows.

Great Musical with the hit song On the Beach

6th July: Hard Day's Night

The Fab Four Film with great songs, the theme song Hard Day's Night, I Should Have Known Better, Can't Buy Me Love, She Loves You. Just some of the brilliant songs.

6th Aug: First Men in the Moon

Starring Lionel Jeffries in a science fiction film of the H. G. Wells Novel.

17th Sept: Goldfinger

The third Bond Movie starring Sean Connery as James Bond.

10th Dec: Carry on Cleo

Starring Sid James as Mark Anthony and Amanda Barrie as Cleopatra, and Kenneth Williams as Julius Caesar.

My order of my favourites from 1964 was:

Zulu

Hard Day's Night

Goldfinger

Carry on Cleo

First Men in the Moon

Dr Strangelove

Wonderful Life

I am listening to the latest hits on the radio from the Rolling Stones with their Little Red Rooster, Petula Clark's Downtown and Val Doonican's Walk Tall, while making my list.

<u>The News Headlines</u>

The British House of Commons has approved an increase in the annual pay rise for Members of Parliament to £3250.

Robbie Brightwell, the Captain of the British Olympic athletics team, married Ann Packer, an Olympic Gold, and Silver medallist.

The British House of Commons vote by 185 majority in favour of total abolition of Capital Punishment.

Donald Campbell broke his own World Water Speed record on Lake Dumbleyung in Western Australia. He achieved an average speed of 276.33 miles per hour over two runs in his jet boat Bluebird.

Death of Field Marshal Lord Wilson, who as Sir Henry Maitland Wilson was Supreme Allied Commander of Mediterranean 1944-45, aged 83.

It's Christmas Eve, 7 o'clock in the evening and I am with my Grandparents, Sister, Ian, and Val.

The house is buzzing with noise as my Mum, Aunties and Uncles and their friends turn up at the house.

The drinks that are on the sideboard are being poured, and the air is full of smoke, with the ashtrays overflowing.

The gathering is the start of the evening as everyone bar us is going out on the town.

It's a very exciting atmosphere.

As everyone started to move out for the night's entertainment, my Mum hung back. She came up to me and reassured me we were going to have a great Christmas, even though Dad was many, many miles away.

She had a present in her hand for me and said I could open it now.

It was a small square shaped package, in bright coloured wrapping paper. I eagerly opened it up.

It was a 45 RPM single. As she walked away, I smiled and waved, thanking her. It was to be a treasured gift.

My cousin's Big Red Dansette Record Player was in the room.

I ran over to it and turned it on. I played the 'B' side first, The Beatles 'She's a Woman'. What a sound. After a couple of times, I then took off the overarm and turned the record over, so I could play the 'A' side time and again.

Everything is good. In fact, in my world, as the Beatles said, you could say "I FEEL FINE."

References

The Grolier Society Limited. (1965). *The Year Book 1965*. Farringdon, London, E.C.4: Fleetway Printers Limited.

References

The Grolier Society Limited. (1965). *The Year Book 1965*.
 Farringdon, London, E.C.4: Fleetway Printers Limited.